BIG PICTURE PRESS

First published in the UK in 2022 by Big Picture Press,
an imprint of Bonnier Books UK
4th Floor, Victoria House
Bloomsbury Square, London WC1B 4DA
Owned by Bonnier Books
Sveavägen 56, Stockholm, Sweden
www.bonnierbooks.co.uk

1 3 5 7 9 10 8 6 4 2

ISBN 978-1-78741-994-0

For Astrid – B.T.
For Otis and Tristan – C.B.

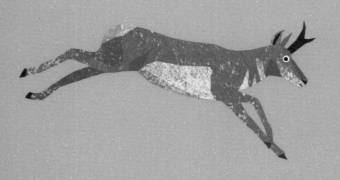

This book was typeset in
Core Circus Rough and Neutraface Text
The illustrations were created digitally

Written by Camilla de la Bedoyere
Edited by Isobel Boston
Designed by Nathalie Eyraud
Production by Ella Holden

Printed in China

MIX
Paper from
responsible sources
FSC® C104723

THERE ARE
MAMMALS
EVERYWHERE

ILLUSTRATED BY BRITTA TECKENTRUP
WRITTEN BY CAMILLA DE LA BEDOYERE

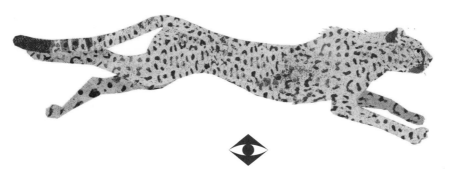

BPP

THERE ARE MAMMALS EVERYWHERE

Mammals live almost everywhere on Earth and they come in an astonishing array of shapes and sizes. Tiny **bumblebee bats**, fluttering through the forest, are smaller than your thumb. The colossal **blue whale** swims in the deep ocean and – at more than 30 metres long – is the largest animal to ever live. But wherever they live and whatever their size, all mammals feed their young with milk.

Bottlenose dolphin

Grey seal

Polar bear

Red kangaroo

Chimpanzee

Brown bear

African lion

Pronghorn

Common warthog

Black rat

Arctic hare

Giant anteater

Meerkat

Short-beaked echidna

Bumblebee bat

Maasai giraffe

African elephant

African rhinoceros

Plains zebra

Black panther

Common hippopotamus

South African cheetah

Crested porcupine

Zorilla

Domestic cat

Some of these mammals are record-breakers! Which mammal do you think is the deadliest to humans? Can you also find the mammal with the best sense of smell, the fastest mammal over a long distance and the mammal that makes the nastiest smell?

IT'S A MAMMAL!
(SO WHAT *IS* THAT?)

There are almost 6,000 species of mammal alive today. Mammals may look very different on the outside, but they all have bony **skeletons** that allow them to perform a wide range of movements. Some mammals have four legs and a tail, but others walk on two legs, fly using two wings, or have flippers and fins.

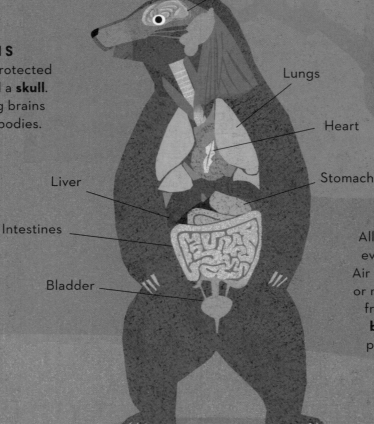

Brain

Lungs

Heart

Liver

Stomach

Intestines

Bladder

BIG BRAINS

A mammal's brain is protected by a bony case called a **skull**. Mammals all have big brains for the size of their bodies.

BREATHING AIR

All mammals use **lungs** to breathe air, even the mammals that live in water. Air reaches the lungs through the nose or mouth and the lungs absorb **oxygen** from it. The oxygen passes into the **blood vessels** and the **heart** then pumps the blood around the body.

RECORD-BREAKERS

Everyone knows that dogs have a superb sense of smell, but it's **polar bears** that have record-breaking snouts. They have been spotted following the scent of **seals** across the ice for over 60 kilometres!

Black rats may not look deadly, but they are more dangerous to humans than any other mammal because they spread disease, including food poisoning and plagues.

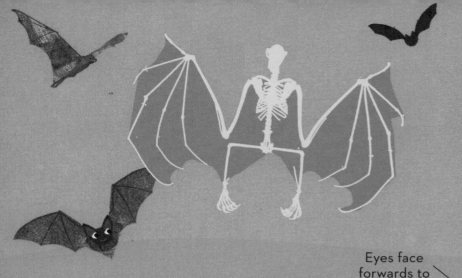

BATS

Bats are the only mammals that have wings and can fly. Their wings are made up of large sheets of leathery skin that are stretched between the long, skinny bones of their front limbs and their legs. The largest bats are huge, with a wingspan of 150 centimetres or more.

Long, bendy spine

Fur is often coloured with spots or stripes to provide **camouflage**

Eyes face forwards to focus on prey

CATS

Members of the **cat** family have strong, bendy bodies that allow them to run, climb and pounce. They have powerful legs and feet that are equipped with claws, and their jaws are lined with sharp teeth. Long tails help them to balance as they quietly stalk their prey.

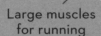

Large muscles for running

Claws for gripping on to the ground or tree bark

SEALS

Seals, **sealions** and **walruses** belong to a group of mammals called **pinnipeds**. They live in water so they have flippers and strong tails for diving and swimming. Pinnipeds have a thick layer of fat, called **blubber**, beneath the skin to keep them warm in chilly seas. Some have furry bodies, but others have smooth skin and whiskers on their snouts.

The fastest mammal over a long distance is actually the **pronghorn**. It can keep up a top speed of 56 kilometres for an hour before it needs a rest.

Many mammals make foul smells to scare other animals away, but a **zorilla** could probably out-stink them all. It sprays a burning liquid from its bottom that smells so terrible even lions turn tail when they see a stripy zorilla nearby!

MAMMALS HAVE BEEN AROUND FOR AGES

Mammals have been around for a really long time. The first mammals looked like **shrews**, which are tiny **mouse-like** animals with long, whiskered snouts. They lived about 210 million years ago, when **dinosaurs** walked the Earth and none of them grew much bigger than a **cat**! When the dinosaurs died out, mammals began to change and evolve into the vast range of creatures that live today.

Morganucodon

210 MILLION YEARS AGO

Morganucodons were amongst the earliest mammals to live. They were small, furry creatures that ate insects.

Elasmotherium

Two million years ago, our human ancestors would have kept a safe distance from this giant rhinoceros! **Elasmotherium** was a plant-eater but it was equipped with a huge, scary horn on its head.

Gigantopithecus

The mighty **Gigantopithecus** was one of the tallest mammals to ever live – reaching an impressive 3 metres in height. This giant ape lived in warm forests one million years ago.

Megatherium

Megatherium grew an incredible 6 metres long. This giant sloth lived 10,000 years ago and used its long claws to reach leaves high up in trees.

Eomaia

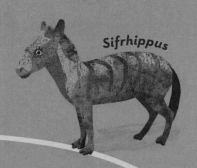

Sifrhippus

Eomaia lived 125 million years ago. It was a long-snouted mammal that grew 10 centimetres long. The babies grew inside their mother's body, just like modern mammals.

The first horses were the size of a cat and ate leaves instead of grass. **Sifrhippus** lived about 50 million years ago, when the world was much warmer than it is today.

Apidium

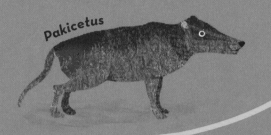

Pakicetus

Monkeys and apes evolved from animals like **Apidium**, which lived 30 million years ago. Apidium jumped from branch to branch, eating fruit and flowers, just like many of its modern relatives.

Forty million years ago, the first whales lived on land, not in the sea! **Pakicetus** probably spent most of its time hunting on land, and occasionally paddled about in shallow water, looking for fish to eat.

Woolly mammoth

Giraffe

Woolly mammoths had long, shaggy fur to keep them warm during the last Ice Age. They went extinct about 5,000 years ago when temperatures increased.

The tallest land animal today is the **giraffe**. It can reach 5 metres in height and uses its long neck to reach the juiciest leaves high up in the trees.

WHY ARE MAMMALS UNIQUE?

Mammals are a large and very successful group of animals. They have been able to spread across the world and survive in all sorts of habitats because they have some impressive ways to stay warm, feed their young and get food.

WARM BLOOD

Mammals are **warm-blooded** – which means they can control their body temperature. This allows them to stay warm even if the weather turns cold, or if they live in cold water. They can also cool themselves down when they get too hot – they often do this by sweating or panting. African elephants flap their huge ears to cool down!

BIG BRAINS

Many mammals are intelligent animals that can play, learn and solve problems. This helps them to develop the skills they need to stay safe from predators and to find food.

FUR

Hairs grow from a mammal's skin, creating a thick fur coat that has many uses. It keeps the mammal warm and its colours and patterns can help to **camouflage** the mammal, so it can hide from predators.

BABIES AND MILK

Almost all mammals give birth to their babies (rather than laying eggs) and feed them with milk that the mother makes in a special part of her body called **mammary glands**. The milk is the perfect food for the babies and it protects them from disease.

SEA OTTERS

Sea otters can be spotted floating in the Pacific Ocean. Their favourite habitat is around a kelp seabed, where the world's largest and fastest-growing seaweed grows. The otters dive below the waves to find shellfish, fish and crabs to eat.

Sea otters have an incredible 125,000 hairs growing from every square centimetre of skin! The hairs are very fine and trap air between each strand. The air keeps the otter warm, like a thick, waterproof blanket. It also works like a life jacket, helping an otter to float.

A sea otter mother gives birth to one baby at a time, called a **pup**. While she floats in the water, she rests the pup on her belly.

3. The sea otter floats on its back and rests the stone on its belly. It bashes the shellfish against the stone until it cracks open.

2. Some shellfish are very tough so the otter also collects a stone from the seabed and swims to the surface.

1. A hungry sea otter uses its hand-like paws to pick **sea urchins** off the **kelp** or shellfish, such as **clams**, from the seabed.

CAN YOU FIND?

Long-spined **sea urchins** eat the giant kelp and damage the sea otters' habitat. How many sea urchins can you spot grazing on the huge fronds of seaweed?

WHERE DO MAMMALS LIVE?

Nearly all species of mammals live on land – about 98 per cent of them. However, there are groups of mammals that spend most, or all, of their lives in water. These include **pinnipeds**, **whales** and **dolphins**. Other groups of mammals are superb swimmers and spend lots of time in the water, but choose to stay on land when they give birth or raise their young.

WHALES

Whales are perfectly adapted to life in the ocean. They have smooth skin and torpedo-shaped bodies that slip easily through the water. They have **flippers** instead of legs and they breathe using blowholes on the top of their heads.

Whale mothers give birth in the ocean. Their babies are called **calves** and they stay close to their mothers while they grow and learn how to find food.

Blue whale babies are enormous and they grow a thousand times faster than a human baby!

BEAVERS

Beavers belong to a group of mammals called **rodents** that have super-strong front teeth. They use these teeth to gnaw trees and branches and use the wood to build their homes in the middle of a pond or slow-flowing river.

A beavers' home is called a **lodge**. It contains rooms, called **chambers**, where young beavers are kept safe from predators.

Beavers are good swimmers. They enter the lodge through tunnels underwater and can stay safe and warm in their home during long, cold winters.

TUNDRA

The land around the Arctic is called the **tundra** and it is famous for its snowy blizzards and blustery winds. It is a difficult place to live – unless you can stay snug inside your own super-thick fur coat. **Musk oxen** have hair that almost touches their toes and they snuggle up next to each other to get the benefit of some buddy-body-warmth!

FORESTS

Tropical forests are packed with tall trees that bloom all year round, producing plenty of fruit for any animals that can reach it. **Orang-utans** spend almost all of their lives in the branches, using their strong arms to climb from tree to tree, following the fruit as it ripens.

DESERTS

Deserts are very dry habitats that experience extreme temperatures. **Bactrian camels** survive desert life by storing food and water as fat inside their two **humps**. They grow thick, shaggy fur for the icy winter, and shed it for the hot summer months.

CAVES

Many species of bat gather together in caves in big groups called **colonies.** They rest during the day by hanging upside-down from the cave ceiling and go hunting at night. Some caves can house more than five million bats!

CAN YOU FIND?

Other animals like to camp out in a beavers' lodge, including **water voles.** Can you find one of these small, furry rodents with a long tail?

THE SAVANNAH

As the sun sets over the African grassland, mammals gather round a waterhole to make the most of the cooler temperatures. This habitat is called the savannah and it is home to many herds of grass-eating mammals, and the **predators** that hunt them.

African rhinoceroses appear bald, apart from some hairs sprouting on their heads and the tufts on their tails, which they use to swat flies away. These huge mammals like to wallow in the mud – it cools them down and dries to a thick layer that protects their skin like sun cream!

Antelopes look like deer, but they are more closely related to the cattle (cow) family. Antelope stomachs have four **chambers**, which help them to digest tough grasses on the savannah.

One of the most peculiar mammals of the savannah is the **aardvark**. It is one of the fastest-burrowing animals in the world and it is rarely seen except at night-time, when it emerges from its den to feast on **ants** and **termites**.

Long-legged pigs, called **warthogs**, run across the savannah, with a row of piglets trotting behind. Warthogs raise their young in burrows that have been dug by **aardvarks**.

CAN YOU FIND?
Giraffes are animals of the savannah, but when they are grazing on leaves they can be hard to see. Can you spot a giraffe's head poking up above some trees?

A group of **hyenas** is called a **clan** and it is led by a female. Hyenas are skilful hunters and even attack large animals such as **elephants** and **buffaloes**.

A family of **lions** is called a **pride**. The female lions in the pride work as a team to hunt **antelope** and **zebra** while the male lion stays with the cubs, relaxing in the shade of an acacia tree.

Hippopotamuses love to wallow in the water during the hot daytime, but at night they emerge onto the land to eat grass.

Small animals on the savannah need to be on the look-out for danger at all times. **Meerkats** hide in burrows underground and stand on mounds to spy **snakes** and other predators.

Zebras belong to the horse family and they live in large herds that feed together, keeping a watchful eye out for predators. Their stripy fur may confuse predators when the herd gallops away.

STAYING ALIVE

Fur is a very useful skin covering. Not only does it keep a mammal warm, and protect the soft skin beneath, it can also come in all sorts of colours and patterns. These colours, stripes, blotches and spots can be used to camouflage an animal, which means it can hide from both **predators** and **prey**.

SHOW-OFFS

In snowy places, such as the Arctic and on mountain-tops, many mammals grow white fur to help them **camouflage** in the winter. In the summer, some of them grow brown or grey fur instead, to help them hide amongst rocks and plants.

CAN YOU FIND?

There are six different mammals hiding in this arctic scene – can you find them all?

MASTERS OF SURVIVAL

SCALES

The soft body of a **Chinese pangolin** is protected by a suit of armour, made of overlapping scales. Its belly and throat have no scales, but they are hidden when the pangolin rolls up into a ball, making it difficult to attack.

HORNS

African buffaloes are big, powerful beasts. If a **lion** attacks a herd of buffaloes, they form a circle around the youngest members of the herd and use their horns to defend themselves. A buffalo's mighty horns can easily stab and slash a lion's skin.

SPINES

The spines of a **porcupine** are actually sharp, stiff hairs, called **quills**. The North American porcupine has 300,000 quills and each one has about 700 tiny **barbs** near its tip. The barbs grip into the flesh of an attacker, and making it very painful to retreat!

BUILD A HOME

Tiny **harvest mice** make easy prey for **birds**, **snakes** and other mammals. They build nests from straw, raised above the ground where they can hide their babies from predators. The nest is the shape of a hollow ball and it's attached to reeds or tall stems of grass.

POISON

Before a **slow loris** leaves her baby to search for food she licks them! She has special places on her elbows that ooze a poison and she licks this poison and spreads it on her baby. It tastes toxic and smells bad, so predators think twice before attacking the youngster.

FEEDING

One of the reasons that mammals are such a successful group of animals is because they have developed some incredible ways to find and eat all sorts of food – from **ants** to **zebras**!

SENSES

Before an animal can eat, it has to find its food. Mammals have superb **senses** such as sight, hearing and smell that are perfect for seeking different sources of food.

When a **star-nosed mole** is on the hunt for juicy **worms** or **snails** to eat it wiggles the 22 soft, fleshy tentacles on its snout. The tentacles detect the smell and movement of other creatures.

A **tarsier's** eyeballs are bigger than its brain! It hunts at night and it needs big eyes to detect as much light as possible in the dark rainforest.

Large ears are perfect for 'catching' sounds and directing them to a mammal's **eardrum**, where the sound is turned into signals that pass to the brain. **Fennec foxes** use their huge ears to listen for the sounds of animals moving beneath the sand.

As a **dolphin** swims, it makes clicking sounds that travel through water and hit the bodies of fish nearby. The sounds bounce back to the dolphin and give it information about the size and position of the fish. This is called **echolocation** and it's such a brilliant system for finding food that many **bats** use it too!

TEETH

Mammals that eat a meat-based diet are called **carnivores** and their teeth need to be good at stabbing, tearing and slicing. **Herbivores** are animals that eat plants and they need teeth that are the perfect shape for snipping leaves and stems and grinding them into a mush that can be easily swallowed.

Tigers have long, dagger-like teeth for stabbing. They are called **fangs**, or **canine teeth**, and can be as long as an adult's finger! They also have **carnassial teeth** on the side of their jaws that fit together like scissor blades to cut chunks of meat.

Sheep mostly eat grass so they need small, sharp **incisors** at the front of their jaw for snipping these tough plants. Large grinding teeth at the back are called **molars**. They have ridges that help grind up the grass.

NO TEETH

Most mammals have teeth, but **anteaters**, **duck-billed platypuses** and some **whales** are toothless.

Most **whales** have cone-shaped teeth for catching **fish** and **squid**, but **baleen whales** have a sieve-like sheets called **baleen plates** instead. When the whale gulps a mouthful of water, the baleen plates work like a sieve to trap small creatures, such as **shrimp**.

Anteaters use their superb sense of smell to sniff out ant nests and termite mounds. They rip them open with their long, curved claws and then scoops up the insects using a very long, sticky tongue. They can devour 35,000 bugs in one day!

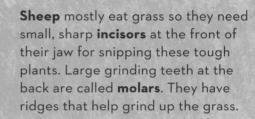

One of the world's strangest mammals is the **duck-billed platypus**. It has a beak-shaped snout that can sense the electrical signals given off by its prey in water.

MOVING

As dawn breaks above an Asian rainforest, and early morning sunlight shines on the tall treetops, two distinctive sounds can be heard: singing and rustling. The **gibbons** are awake and on the move!

Gibbons are a type of tailless monkey, called an **ape**. A gibbon is rightly known as the king of the swingers because this ape can race through the trees, swinging from branch to branch. Gibbons also leap long distances travelling more than 10 metres in a single jump.

To travel through the jungle, gibbons use their hands to grip branches and swing their bodies to move through trees. This type of movement is called **brachiation**:

CAN YOU FIND?
Gibbons make a move when there are predators about. Can you spot a hungry **black eagle** that is lurking in the jungle?

1. Holding on tight to the branch with one hand, the gibbon swings its body forward.

2. The gibbon's body swings round so the second arm can reach out.

3. The gibbon's hand grabs the next branch and the first arm now reaches forward.

When gibbons want to talk to each other they sing songs that echo through the jungle. Their beautiful love-duets – performed by a male and female to one another – sound like eerie whoops and wails.

4. When the gibbon is ready to stop, it uses a foot to grip a lower branch and steady its body.

RECORD-BREAKERS

The fastest runners over a short distance are **cheetahs**. They can achieve top speeds of 87 kilometres an hour when chasing **antelope**, but can only run for about 60 seconds before they get too hot. A cheetah's long tail helps it to balance as it turns corners and it uses its claws to grip the ground, like the spikes on an athlete's running shoes.

Being bouncy is a surprisingly good way of moving at speed – and leaping out of danger! **Red kangaroos** can jump up to 12 metres in a single bound, and reach heights of 3 metres to leap over fences.

MAMMAL PARENTS

Most mammal mothers keep their young inside their bodies while they grow – all except for two very strange groups: **monotremes** lay eggs and **marsupials** raise their babies in pouches.

EGG-LAYING MAMMALS

There are just five species of mammal that lay eggs: four species of **echidna** and just one species of **duck-billed platypus**.

Echidnas can grow up to 100 centimetres long. They have short legs, a long snout and tiny eyes and they have spines growing between strands of hair. Some echidnas lay a single egg in a **burrow**, but others keep their egg in a **pouch**.

MAMMALS WITH POUCHES

There are about 300 species of **marsupial** and, like the **monotremes**, many of them live in or around Australia. **Koalas, kangaroo, quolls, wombats** and **oppossums** are all types of marsupial.

A kangaroo **joey** stays in its mother's pouch for several months as it grows, although it may climb out from time to time to stretch its legs!

Mother kangaroos give birth to tiny babies, called **joeys**, which are often no bigger than a jellybean. A joey must make its own way to the mother's **pouch**, where it latches on to a teat and suckles on its mother's milk.

PARENTING SKILLS: GREY WOLVES

Grey wolves live in large family groups called **packs**. The leaders of the pack are called the **alpha female** and **alpha male**.

In **Spring**, the alpha female chooses a male to mate with. The two wolves nuzzle each other, touching noses and grooming each other's fur. The wolves form a close bond that lasts for a lifetime.

At **seven months old**, the playful pups are allowed to join the pack on hunting trips. They watch the adults to learn how to find, chase and kill prey.

The alpha female is pregnant for about **60 days** and she uses this time to dig a **den** where she will hide her **pups**. During the pregnancy, four to six pups grow inside their mother's body, in a special place called a **uterus**.

When the pups are **four weeks old**, they are brave enough to leave the den and explore. They now have teeth and can start to eat meat.

Pups are born blind and deaf, but they have a good sense of smell. The mother feeds them with milk but other females in the pack can also make milk and take over feeding when the mother wants a rest.

The whole pack helps to care for the growing pups and they even babysit when the alpha wolves go hunting.

MALI ELEPHANTS

In the hot desert lands of Mali in Africa, **elephant** families set out on an epic journey each year in search of food and water. Only by working as a team and taking care of each other, can these huge mammals survive in this harshest of habitats.

A baby elephant – a **calf** – lies in the mud to cool down. Calves are cared for by their mothers, aunts, cousins and siblings. They stroke the baby, or gently slap it with their trunks if it moves too far from the safety of the herd.

There has been no rain for some time, so the land is dry and the plants are dying. It is time for the herd to move west. They start a journey that will cover about 500 kilometres, much of it in blistering heat and sudden sandstorms.

At the beginning of the **dry season**, herds of elephants roam along marshes, just south of Timbuktu. There is water and some small trees grow here, where the desert sands start to spread across the land.

When the rainy season is over, the elephants will continue their circular route, back to where they began in the marshes of the north.

A female elephant, called the **matriarch**, leads the herd. She is old and can remember the route she must take, and she knows how to search for water, scanning the sky for signs of rain clouds.

The elephants reach Lake Banzena where they rest, seeking shade in thickets of trees while they wait for the rainy season to begin. They can talk to each other by making low rumbling sounds that travel long distances through the ground. Elephants hear and feel the rumbles through their feet!

The grey clouds on the horizon tell the elephants that rains are falling in the south, and they begin the next stage of their trek. Their traditional route takes them through villages that have been built in the area, so now they must walk even further to avoid the villagers.

The elephants have to travel quickly so they can reach the rains before they die of thirst or starvation. Young elephants are helped along by their family, and allowed to rest in the shade of their larger bodies.

Finally, the herd reaches the lush grasslands of Boni. The **rainy season** has turned the land green, with plants springing up everywhere. The waterholes are full again, and the elephants can play together in the water, enjoying a well-earned rest.

CAN YOU FIND?

Elephants produce lots of poo, or **dung**. **Dung beetles** collect the dung, roll it into balls and lay their eggs in it. When the eggs hatch, the **grubs** eat the dung. How many dung beetles can you find?

MAMMALS AND PEOPLE

The lives of mammals have been intertwined with humans since the earliest times. For many thousands of years, people have hunted mammals for meat and used their skins and furs. **Cattle**, **camels**, **llamas** and **horses** have been used to plough the land or carry people and their goods far across the globe.

PEOPLE AND PETS
Wild **cats** may have been tamed, or **domesticated**, more than 10,000 years ago! The first **dogs** lived among humans even earlier, when **wolves** were used on hunting trips during the last Ice Age. Today, cats and dogs are still much-loved companions.

MAMMALS AT WORK
Some mammals have been trained to do important tasks. **Assistance dogs** help people who cannot see or hear, or who have difficulties with moving. Life-saving **rats** have been trained to sniff out bombs in war zones and **mice** have learned how to find dangerous drugs that pass through airports.

MYTHS AND LEGENDS
All over the world, people have put mammals at the centre of their stories. These include flying **horses**, such as **Pegasus** from the Greek myths. Some world religions revere mammals such as **cattle**, **bears** and **elephants**, and honour them in festivals and ceremonies.

HUMANS ARE MAMMALS TOO

Humans belong to the group of mammals called **primates**, which includes **monkeys** and **apes**. We are similar to our primate cousins in many ways!

Like humans, **monkeys** and **apes** have hands and use them to grip, hold, throw and pick up small things. **Chimps** poke sticks into termite mounds then pull them out to lick the bugs.

MAMMALS IN DANGER

Mammals are an essential part of the natural world, but they are in greater danger than ever before. In modern times, 85 species of mammal have already gone **extinct**, and nearly a quarter of all mammal species are now at risk.

There are possibly fewer than 10 **vaquitas** left in the world. These rare river porpoises have died out due to **pollution** and also due to getting trapped in fishing nets. It's hoped that the last few can be saved, before it is too late.

No one has seen a wild **scimitar-horner oryx** in its desert home since 1988. These majestic beasts were hunted for their horns and now they are kept safe behind fences. Hopefully one day they can be released back into the wild.

Cotton-top tamarins live in the forests of South America, but is thought only 2,000 of them still survive there. In the past, they were sold as pets, and their habitat has been removed to build homes for people instead. Scientists and local people are now working hard to save them.

The shrinking jungles of Sumatra, an island in Southeast Asia, are home to fewer than 80 **rhinos**. Their forests have been cut down to make way for farms and they are hunted for their horns. The last Sumatran rhinos are now kept safe and protected from hunters.

Human childhood is a time of play and learning. The childhood of an **orang-utan** lasts for about seven years, and during this time the mother cares for her youngster and teaches it how to find the best fruits to eat.

Primates are experts at communicating. They use sounds to talk, but they also use their faces to show how they are feeling. **Chimps** pout and whimper when they are feeling unhappy and when they are happy they make a special smile, with their lower teeth showing.